GEOFFREY GRIGSON

HENRY MOORE

PENGUIN BOOKS

THE PENGUIN MODERN PAINTERS
Editor Sir Kenneth Clark

First published 1944
Reprinted 1944, 1946, 1951

Colour plates made and printed by John Swain & Son Ltd, Barnet, Herts
Text pages printed by Hazell, Watson & Viney Ltd, Aylesbury, Bucks
Published by Penguin Books Ltd, Harmondsworth, Middlesex
Made and printed in Great Britain

HENRY MOORE

HENRY MOORE is now 53 years old. He was born in Yorkshire, a Yorkshireman, the son of a Yorkshire coalminer, in 1898. So he was 16 when the Great War began, and he served in his eighteenth and nineteenth years. When he came out of the army he knew what he was going to be. He had intended to be a sculptor ever since childhood. The first sculptor he heard of was Michelangelo. He had been told Vasari's story of Michelangelo and the head of the Old Fawn, how someone joked that old men usually had a tooth or two missing, and how Michelangelo, who was 14, took this earnestly, and at once knocked a stone tooth out of the copy he had made, and tidied up the carving of the mouth and gum. This story, heard when he was 10 or 11, shaped Henry Moore's determination to be a sculptor; and he was also much impressed as a child by the carvings he saw whenever he went into Methley church.

When he was demobilized, then, and went to the Leeds School of Art, in 1919, he clearly, confidently maintained his intention. He soon found himself unsatisfied by the normal academic training in sculpture, and by the classical models which stood round to be drawn and copied. He was lucky: for one thing, in the Leeds Reference Library he came across Roger Fry's book, *Vision and Design*. In this way he first learned of Negro and Mexican sculpture. Then students could also go and see Sir Michael Sadler's collection at Leeds, and for the first time Moore examined paintings by Gaugin and Van Gogh. Roger Fry's book led him to other books on Negro and ancient sculpture of all kinds, and also gave him the clue to the British Museum. Saying that museums or galleries are useless, that they kill pictures or sculpture, is a trick, a snobbish trick, handed down from the rich dilettante of a past age. In museums and galleries, for instance, an artist can pick and choose and defend himself against academies and schools of art. And this is what Henry Moore did in the British Museum, when he came from Leeds to London, to the Royal College of Art. He has never underrated the value of his academic training. He enjoyed drawing and modelling from the life, and he valued the repertory of forms they gave him. But he also wanted to carve. Carving was not encouraged at the R.C.A., but Moore conceived that the real tradition of sculpture enjoined the hard control and the energy of direct carving. He saw this for himself in the sculpture galleries and the heaped-up ethnological glass cases of the British Museum, where he spent most of his week-ends during his first half-year in London. Making a selection from the muddle of crowded carvings in the ethnological cases was a critical, enlivening act of self-discovery. Away from the college Moore had already begun to carve, and he was now beginning to know the more elemental and lively sculpture being made in Europe. In Paris, for example, Brancusi was carving his tense and rather sleek units of life.

The next thing Moore did was to win the R.C.A. travelling scholarship. It took him abroad for six months. Italy has not always had a good effect on English artists, but Moore went there clear in his mind that he was not going to be captured by the Renaissance. He was after the simple, monumental forms of life. He found them, above all, in the remaining chapel of Santa Maria del Carmine at Florence, in the solemn, solid figures grouped on the walls by Masaccio. He made copies from Masaccio. He made it a rite to go to the church for half an hour every day, before doing anything else; and he stood looking at these frescoes, which were more lively and monumental, and assured, and wonderful than anything he had yet seen. Raphael, Michelangelo, and others had gone to the same place, and Vasari wrote: 'All the most celebrated sculptors since Masaccio's day have become excellent and illustrious by studying their art in this chapel.'

II

Many other artists have influenced Henry Moore – Giotto, Blake, Turner, Picasso. He has seen many other things, such as the palaeolithic cave paintings in Spain, but he has most of all been moved by these Masaccio paintings (which he keeps still in his mind), and by the hard solemnity of Mexican sculpture. Masaccio's figures and Mexican carvings are in many ways not unlike. In both, detail gives way to monumentality and strength. In both, features are made simple and subordinate. Both are grand without dictatorial swagger. Both combine deliberation with a held-in immensity of life. That life, that held-in, immense life, is Moore's interest. He is interested in the rounded, solid shapes into which life builds itself. And when he came back from Italy, Moore became a pilgrim also to the Natural History Museum. In the

British Museum he had seen the carved symbols of life, in the other he now saw life in its natural forms and framework, from the cells to the skeleton. Saying 'life' we often mean, especially when discussing writing and art, only human life – not human form and movement in opposition to the form and movement of a dog or a fish, but human beings thinking, feeling, desiring, arranging, and so on. This is not the life of Moore's sculpture. His beings are not springing and leaping, or else brooding in conscious expression of some ideal. His interest is not for heroes, or harmonious perfection, or gods. In some of his Tube-shelter drawings, for instance, his women are tortoise-headed, or pin-headed. They have not the heads of Madonnas, or angels, or a governess by Chardin. Moore has never been attracted by the fag-end of the old ideal values of Renaissance Europe. In art, these values have decayed into a set form. In sculpture, the Renaissance Christ has been smoothed into the plaster Christ of the Catholic church-furnisher (in the Church of England sculptural passion has become taste-controlled by diocesan advisory committees), and the old ideas of nobility and sacrifice have become a howitzer squatting at Hyde Park Corner like a petrified toad, and the hero has become a Cabinet Minister on a pedestal, in bronze boots. What sculpture needed in this country was to be thought out again, or re-explored by feeling. So back to life, or the simple, rounded forms of life. Back to seeing everything. Back to the Natural History Museum, as well as to Mexican sculpture and Masaccio.

Henry Moore has made several statements about his own carvings in their relation to bones, shells, pebbles, and so on, and also in their relation to the religious carving of the Mexicans, the Sumerians, the Egyptians, and the Negroes.

'Primitive art ... makes a straightforward statement, its primary concern is with the elemental, and its simplicity comes from direct and strong feeling.'

'The most striking quality common to all primitive art is its intense vitality. It is something made by people with a direct and immediate response to life.'

'Sumerian sculpture shows a richness of feeling for life and its wonder and mystery.'

But remember, when you look at the shapes cut and smoothed by Henry Moore, that these early peoples, in whose carvings the sense of living form was so strong, had an actual pictorial knowledge of life much less detailed and extensive than our own. They saw life in the form of large organisms, brute or man. We see it also in the plates and diagrams of a biological text-book. Rounded shapes by Moore may be related to a breast, or a pear, or a bone, or a hill, or a pebble shaped among other pebbles on a shingle bar. But they might also relate to the curves of a human embryo, to an ovary, a sac, or to a single-celled primitive organism. Revealed by anatomy or seen with a microscope, such things are included now in our visual knowledge. Art, or the forms of art, change with such knowledge. In the eighteenth century Stubbs painted an exquisite bunch of flowers held in a woman's hand up to the nostrils of one of his anatomically correct horses. Botanical classification and research and interest in gardening helped to make flowers an especial object under eighteenth-century eyes. An eighteenth-century physiologist investigated the way in which a sunflower follows the sun, so Blake and other writers used images about the sunflower. Humphry Davy gave lectures on science; Coleridge went to them to 'increase his stock of metaphor'. In our age the discovery and study of single-celled organisms has been followed by a search after the units, the source, the primitive form of expression; and no artist can live by himself, or live altogether in, or by, the impressions once vivid in the eyes of a dead generation. So when some critics (critics are very often stuck fast in the record of old impressions) talk persistently of the distorted vision and the disordered mind of contemporary art, they are simply showing the restrictions of their own experience. Academic critics will not be familiar with the cells and organs and elements of life if they read only Plato and Jane Austen, look only at a lion by Rubens, and a lady by Gainsborough. Biology must also be acknowledged; and some of the dislike of what painters and sculptors do at the present time certainly does come from this restriction, does come from a narrow, negative sixth-form and university education in the half inhuman humanities. To be interested in life, as Moore is, rather below the conscious level, is not to be sub-human. The rounded limbs of a human foetus, a fertilized egg, or the heart of a water flea, or even the pneumococcus that chokes and ruins lungs with pneumonia, would not, when realized with the bigness of life, be less worthy than a lounge suit in white marble or an Alsatian dog a million times smoothly reproduced in coloured china.

All the same it is not so easy to value Moore's big sense of the wonder and mystery of universal life. When I look at his carvings I sometimes have to reflect that so much of our visual experience of the anatomical details and microscopical forms of life comes to us, not direct, but through the biologist. Microscopical forms are as 'big' as any other forms, but the 'intense vitality' of primitive art was given to carvings because the carvers had a direct knowledge of animals as vehicles of life, alert, walking, leaping, and at rest. I do not say that Moore's pantheism is a motive as exalted as the vision of human life in Raphael's *School of Athens* or Michelangelo's two sonnets –

Heaven-born, the soul a heavenward course must hold;
Beyond the visible world she soars to seek,
(For what delights the sense is false and weak)
Ideal Form, the universal mould,

and so on. Moore's pantheism is not Goethe's or Wordsworth's. Moore does not play up Nature as a beauty. His carvings by no means always reach the grandeur of life. Big without being pompous, the life he carves, you might say, has only the virtue sometimes of not being dead. But that is one virtue up on a lip-service to humanism coupled with a sly and silent support of the robber principles of modern society. Life as life is simply a beginning, an honest beginning. And this life is not by any means the whole of Henry Moore's art. The only vision in art, or feeling in art, is an embodied feeling. Let us see how Moore's vision is bodied out in his sculpture and, particularly, in his drawings.

III

In Gloucester Cathedral, screens and arches of stone, thrown across the interior, create depth, create ordered images of eternity and infinity. At one place thin stone ribs leap up with superb skill to meet, at a sharp, tense point of spiritual contact, a strut thrusting down from the roof. Here is the builders' intellect brilliantly interpreting the mysteries of religion. In the limestone cliffs of the Gower peninsula a huge wall, cut through with windows and a door, closes in a narrow, tall cleft, inside which the rock twists into fantastic forms. The rock swirls, and a hollow communicates with another hollow through a deep hole. In the cathedral, a religious mystery; in the cleft, or cave, a natural mystery, emphasized by man. Come down in scale. Outside the cave there is a beach of pebbles, some of grey, some of pink limestone, ground into different rounded shapes, cut into with hollows, or pierced with holes. The pebble is a cave in the round, and the pebble and the cleft are types of the art of Henry Moore. Analogies are at once obvious: the darkness of the womb, and shapes swelling and thrusting from it; the bony structure of ribs, the round socket of eyes. Eyes in bone, the heart in bone, the embryo in a nook among bones. Or think of another series, the phallus, the tree, the erect posture of human beings, the standing stones of Avebury, the stone images more precisely carved on the slopes of Easter Island, the tapering of the spire of Salisbury Cathedral, or of an obelisk, or of a peak in the Julian

Alps. Anything solid that can show the 'wonder and mystery' of life appeals to Henry Moore. But his interest is somewhere above the type, in between the cave (or Tube tunnel) and the cathedral, the pebble and the perfect ball, the megalith at Avebury, roughly shaped by the people who put it up, and the cathedral spire. Something still and ordered in the fecundity and muddle of life. His tendency is to humanize rock or wood or bone or geological shape, or biological specimen. That compromise produces some of the most monumental, but also at times some of the least moving of Moore's work. His stony reclining landscape women need to be nearer women, very often, or else farther from them; more natural or else more abstract. But his love of the cave and hollow and deep carving gives him room for all kinds of subtlety. His objects of life may be still – a kidney cannot throw a discobolus or hold tables of law – his objects may sprawl, but his scale is always big and he arranges with moving intricacy mass against hollow, hollow against line, and height and breadth. That, after all, is one element by which painting and sculpture have satisfied and delighted human beings all through history and all through changes of style and subject. Compare a Tube-shelter drawing, for example the *Four Grey Sleepers* (No. 32), with Raphael's *Three Graces* (illustrated in the Phaidon Press book on Raphael). However the two visions differ, the means are exactly the same. In Raphael's three standing figures, the dance of the arms, the heads, the legs, the breasts; in Moore's four sleepers, the solemn, monumental rhythm of the blanket shapes, each stretching outwards from the head, lying like stones on the ground, the rhythm of head against head differently turned, arm against arm, dark depth against depth. Moore has written of the sculptor's need to 'think of, and use form in its full spatial completeness', to think of the solid shape 'whatever its size, as if he were holding it completely enclosed in the hollow of his hand.' And it is necessary, he says, 'to feel shape simply as shape, not as description or reminiscence.' But he also admits that forms have their meaning: 'rounded forms convey an idea of fruitfulness, maturity.' So, like the great inventors, Moore balances his road in between the theorem and the heart. Why else does an early painter set up a crucifix in an agony of rocks and skulls, or a painter of the eighteen-hundreds square up a lime-kiln in a wild valley, or extend the arc of a rainbow across the fertile medley of a landscape? Why else the circle and rectograms of Stonehenge in the desolate spread of Salisbury Plain?

In the mess and muddle and fecundity of life which he finds wonderful and mysterious, Moore puts together shapes by which all that life is both ordered and symbolized.

IV

Sculpture is a severe drill for an artist. No man can jot down the sudden illumination, the harmonious, momentary blend of experiences, by the immediate hacking out of a piece of stone. He cannot carve very well from Nature. He can do these things in oil paint, easier still in ink or pencil or chalk, or in water-colour. (That surely is a reason for the Romantic development of water-colour in an age of originality and spontaneity and truth to Nature, when it was held that 'a thought conceived in the first warmth, an effect with which we are struck at the first view, is never so well expressed as by the strokes that are drawn at that instant.' The answer was water-colour, and the later manipulation of water-colour for intricate detail across a large area was decidedly the cleverness of perversion.) A sculptor can pinch his flash of experience into wax or into clay, but he will not be inclined to do that, if he believes that he must feel in the material he uses, wood or stone. It is better to draw.

'At one time, whenever I made drawings for sculpture, I tried to give them as much the illusion of real sculpture as I could – that is, I drew by the method of illusion, of light falling on a solid object.' This stoniness or woodenness of drawing was less alien to the slow carving of the final object than the pinching and dabbing of such an opposite, soft material as clay. Later Moore found it dangerous to make his drawings too much a 'substitute for sculpture'. The sculpture was 'likely to become only a dead realization of the drawing', so he put down his three-dimensional vision on paper without all the three-dimensional illusions. He draws, all the same, 'mainly as a help towards making sculpture', tapping himself, in his own words, for the first idea, sorting out ideas, developing them, realizing ideas he hasn't time to realize more solidly, and recording from Nature. But he also admits drawing for the enjoyment of drawing. A sign of the artist with great ability is that he can translate the first recorded flash into the more considered, better ordered perfection of the final painting or the final carving, with the flash undiminished and a strength added to it. Sickert once said, unromantically and truly, that 'the sketches of a sketcher are separated by a gulf from those of the painter of pictures.' But the ability to draw, to make a powerful and appealing use of line, always will be a major indication of an artist's rank and vision. Moore is one of the few living artists I know of who can scarcely put down a line without giving it life and interest, and a reason for this is that Nature is attractive to him: that he can see into natural objects. Light, for most of us, is the most effective of all black-outs. It reveals so many familiar aspects to us that we cease to notice the rest of the outside world. Moore reminds me of a deep-sea fish found off one of the Dutch spice islands. These fish have head-lamps of luminous bacilli near their eyes, and the light can be shut on and off at will. Moore doesn't just see: he sees in his own light. He sees everything, the scratch on the bone, the curvature of hills, the graining of bark; he sees into qualities and relation of objects, roundness, depth, darkness, surface, colour, solidity, everything, by means of his own light. He can shut his own light off, or, rather, he can turn it inwards, and ponder within himself over the things it has revealed. An artist so thoroughly possessed by vision records something of it simply by making any considered mark on a piece of paper. In the corners and unemphatic parts of the drawings and paintings of such men, when working at their best, there are no strokes or spots without rhythm, meaning, life, and interest. In many drawings reproduced in this book this masterly quality is evident. No dullness, nothing emptily and carelessly unrealized. Compare the zig-zagging lines of the floor (any section of it as full as most abstract paintings of our time) and the veining of the right-hand pillars in Raphael's *Fire in the Borgo*.

All this is true of Moore's drawings for sculpture as well as his drawings for drawing, or the enjoyment of drawing. Drawing as an end has been somewhat forced upon him, I think, by the war. For one thing, stone could not be so easily transported, either to his studio, or from his studio to exhibitions. The drawings have gained from this. In his earlier, more elaborate drawings in which figures of life establish themselves out of uncertainty and darkness (for example, Plates 7 and 14), he had been able to record a whole, more intricate and extensive in scale than can very well be contained in isolated objects of stone. In these drawings the stones have been erect in their setting of landscape and emotion. But they have been drawings in between idea and hard carving. To war-time drawings, such as the *Four Grey Sleepers* again, he has given back some of the stoniness and depth that he had guarded against in drawings meant for sculpture. Here we can thrust the arms of our sight in among forms in an almost 'full spatial completeness'. Here in these shelter drawings, or in No. 27 or No. 31, most of the sculptor and all of the draughtsman have been at work; and the deep figures in their setting are not just figures of life; they are figures of life (at least, in the Tube series), the wonder of which is terrifically threatened. The figures still belong to the mass of life; they are below the edge of will. Rather than life vertebrate, active and thinking, they are life to which things (terrible things) are being done. Moore has also been forced by the subject of the Tube shelter and coal-mining drawings nearer to the natural proportions of men and women. This is a gain, just as, under other circumstances, a move away from his stony human compromise towards completer abstraction has also been a gain. In fact, in the latest drawings illustrated here, Moore is moving back towards sculpture and asserting once more that he is not bound to any original. The way Moore develops and changes, moving on from one position to another like this, also proves his curiosity and power. He has been influenced by one thing and another, Masaccio and Mexican sculpture, Picasso and cathedral carvings, the effect of natural forces upon stone, English medieval pottery, etc., but he has always kept and developed his own idiom. He has never got stuck in one phase, or made a habit of repeating himself until style has become a manner. He is always on the move.

V

But colour. I have not spoken of Henry Moore's colour, preferring to keep that, a bit artificially, until last. Colour should be, and certainly is with Moore, an extension of drawing. Just as an artist of vision cannot often record a stroke without quality, so he cannot keep feeling and experience, and himself, out of his intimations of tone and colour. A clear way of describing the relation and dance of colour has never been worked out, I suppose partly because we inherit the notion that colour is sensuality and pomp and vanity, and not a first thing to be considered in the putting together and ordering of a picture. But colour has regained honour with us since the eighteenth century. Then, when mathematics and order were the prime interests, colours were subdued and browns and greys had their day. The university don, as often, years behind the time, wrote in 1817: 'The delightful green of Nature cannot be represented in a picture. . . . Nature must be stripped of her green livery, and dressed in the browns of the painters, or confined to her own autumnal tints, in order to be transferred to the canvas.' But when reason, or the conduct of human understanding, began to give way to enthusiasm and spontaneity, when mathematical began to give way to natural sciences, colour, and, in particular, water-colour, with its scope, vividness and speed, began to come in, with the injunction to honour originality, the first idea, and Nature. First colour comes in flatly, clearly, and thinly, as a combination of smooth tints. Think of Rowlandson or Stubbs. In various degrees colour then was an adjunct of drawing. It gains richness and sparkle, developing into a medium. Think of taffeta in Reynolds (whose drawing, it was said, lay under his paint) or in Gainsborough. Think of colour in such poets as Mickle or Chatterton:

> The yellowe broom, where chirp the linnets gay,
> Waves round the cave; and to the blue-streaked skyes
> A shattered rock towres up in fragments gray.

In much of the loveliest and most balanced painting of romantic landscape, for example, in the church walls and windows of Cotman, the water-colours of Turner, the open and shut weather of Constable, colour, as a record of personal exuberance, strikes a bargain with colour as a record of Nature. But in a really good water-colour by Cotman, for example, the colours have their exquisite relation to each other, their quality, and their character as drawing. No point or patch of colour is without the interest of personal quality. The colours also fulfil the subject in a harmony of feeling. Later on, for example, in some pre-Raphaelite painting, this agreement and harmony disappear. You get, say, three pictures in one, a subject without true relation to its drawing, and drawing and subject without true relation to the colours, which are there simply as an accurate transscript. The lovely effectiveness of colour in drawings by Henry Moore is much fed, of course, from his appetite for the colours in Nature, the lichen on the grey rock, the coloured texture of weather-worn stone, the fiery black and red of igneous formations or burning coal, and so on. But because he is so much free of having to say yes to objects, so he is more or less free of having to bargain with the colour of objects. His objects, his line, his ordering, freely represent his vision of life; by his colours he is freely represented as well. So in English art his nearer relations are not Cotman or Constable so much as Blake and James Ward and Turner. He admires James Ward's *Bull* and *Gordale Scar*. He admires Turner for his bigness and energy, and as a painter of coloured abstraction, and tornado, and water-spout. Moore's colour, as in Blake's *Newton*, is a free, personal, expressive colour, which also helps and fills out the design. And Blake stands near the beginning of a process working down to Chirico and Picasso and Wyndham Lewis, and Moore himself, and Graham Sutherland, a process which comes at last to a personal freedom of colour in an art which is, or nearly is, abstract.

In some coloured drawings by Moore I feel the colour as a bait to the eye, a very attractive bait, icing, cherries, and angelica on shapes for sculpture.

But his deepest drawings are right, and full of surprise, in their colour, which speaks as an indivisible part of the total effect, the total meaning, his entire view of the 'wonder and mystery' of life. Most of his drawings may simply be for sculpture; but I am not sure, much as he will dislike the idea, that Moore's claim on us does not really derive from the freedom and big splendour of his best drawings as much as from every piece of stone and wood he has ever carved. But there would be no drawings without the carving, no carvings without the drawing.

There is a statement which fits the work of Henry Moore:

Nature is played out as a Beauty, but not as a Mystery . . . I don't want to see the original realities – as optical effects, that is. I want to see the deeper reality underlying the scenic, the expression of what are sometimes called abstract imaginings.

And it was made by Thomas Hardy many years ago.

GEOFFREY GRIGSON

COLOUR PLATES

1. *Standing Figures* (Ideas for Wooden Sculpture). 1940. 10¾ × 14½ inches. Chalk, water-colour and pen. Owned by Mrs Ursula Goldfinger.

3. *Platform Scene* (Sleeping People – Sketch Book). 1941. 5½ × 6½ inches. Water-colour and pen. Owned by Artist.

5. *Drawing for Sculpture*. 1937. 15 × 22 inches. Water-colour. Owned by Eric Gregory, Esq.

7. *Drawing for Stone Figures*. 1937. 16 × 21 inches. Water-colour. Owned by Geoffrey Grigson, Esq.

9. *Ideas for Sculpture* (Sketch Book). 1941. 9 × 7 inches. Chalk and water-colour. Owned by Artist.

11. *Two Women Seated*. 1940. 11 × 15 inches. Chalk, water-colour and pen. Owned by Sir Kenneth Clark.

13. *Seated Figure and Pointed Forms*. 1940. 17 × 10 inches. Chalk and water-colour. Owned by Miss Lee Miller.

15. *Landscape with Figures*. 1939. 15 × 17¾ inches. Water-colour. Owned by Mrs Edward Carter.

17. *Figures in a Setting*. 1942. 19 × 24 inches. Chalk, water-colour and pen. Owned by Joseph Pulitzer, Junr, St Louis, Missouri, U.S.A.

19. *Red Rocks and Reclining Figure*. 1942. 15 × 22 inches. Chalk and water-colour. Owned by Philip L. Goodwin, New York.

21. *Figures under a Bank*. 1942. 22 × 17 inches. Chalk, water-colour and pen. Owned by James J. Sweeney, New York.

23. *Draped Figures in Shelter*. 1941. 12½ × 22 inches. Water-colour and pen. Owned by Julian Huxley, Esq.

25. *Tube Shelter Perspective*. 1941. 18¾ × 17 inches. Water-colour and pen. Owned by the Tate Gallery.

27. *Two Women and Child in Shelter*. 1940. 10 × 17 inches. Chalk, water-colour and pen. Owned by Stephen Spender, Esq.

29. *Pink and Green Sleepers*. 1941. 12⅝ × 21¼ inches. Chalk, water-colour and pen. Owned by the Tate Gallery.

31. *Study for Reclining Figure in Wood*. 1940. 7 × 11 inches. Water-colour and pen. Owned by Sir Kenneth Clark.

BLACK-AND-WHITE PLATES

2. *Drawing* (Standing Woman). 1930. 22×15 inches. Chalk and wash. Private Collection.
4. *Figure on Steps*. 1930. 15×22 inches. Water-colour. Owned by Michael Ventris, Esq.
6. *Drawing*. 1933. 11×15 inches. Water-colour and pen. Private Collection.
8. *Drawing from Life* (Seated Figure). 1935. 22×15 inches. Brush and wash drawing. Owned by Michael Ventris, Esq.
10. *Shapes in Bone* (Drawing for Sculpture). 1932. 12½×10 inches. Pencil. Owned by Artist.
12. *Seated Figures for Stone Sculpture*. 1934. 15×22 inches. Charcoal and pen. Owned by Mrs John W. Matthews, Junr, Jenkin Town, Pa., U.S.A.
14. *Standing Stones in Landscape*. 1936. 22×15 inches. Wash and pen. Owned by William C. Ohly, Esq.
16. *Drawing*. 1935. 15×22 inches. Water-colour and pen. Private Collection.
18. *Two Women* (Drawing for Sculpture, combining Wood and Metal). 1939. 20×15 inches. Water-colour. Owned by Sir Kenneth Clark.
20. *Objects* (String and Wood). 1938. 15×22 inches. Charcoal, wash and pen. Private Collection.
22. *Reclining Figure*. 1938. 15×22 inches. Chalk, wash and pen. Owned by Sir Kenneth Clark.
24. *Page of Heads* (Ideas for Sculpture). 1940. 11×15 inches. Water-colour and pen. Owned by Peter Watson, Esq.
26. *Three Women and a Child*. 1940. 7×10 inches. Chalk and water-colour. Owned by Mrs Valentine Dobrée.
28. *Miners at Work on the Coal Face*. 1942. 13½×22 inches. Chalk, wash and pen. The Whitworth Art Gallery, Manchester.
30. *Arrangement of Figures*. 1942. 13½×22 inches. Chalk, wash and pen. Owned by Irina Moore.
32. *Four Grey Sleepers*. 1941. 17×20 inches. Wash and pen. Owned by the Wakefield Art Gallery.

PLATE I STANDING FIGURES (IDEAS FOR WOODEN SCULPTURE) 1940

PLATE 2 DRAWING (STANDING WOMAN) 1930

PLATE 3 PLATFORM SCENE (SLEEPING PEOPLE – SKETCH BOOK) 1941

PLATE 4 FIGURE ON STEPS 1930

PLATE 5 DRAWING FOR SCULPTURE 1937

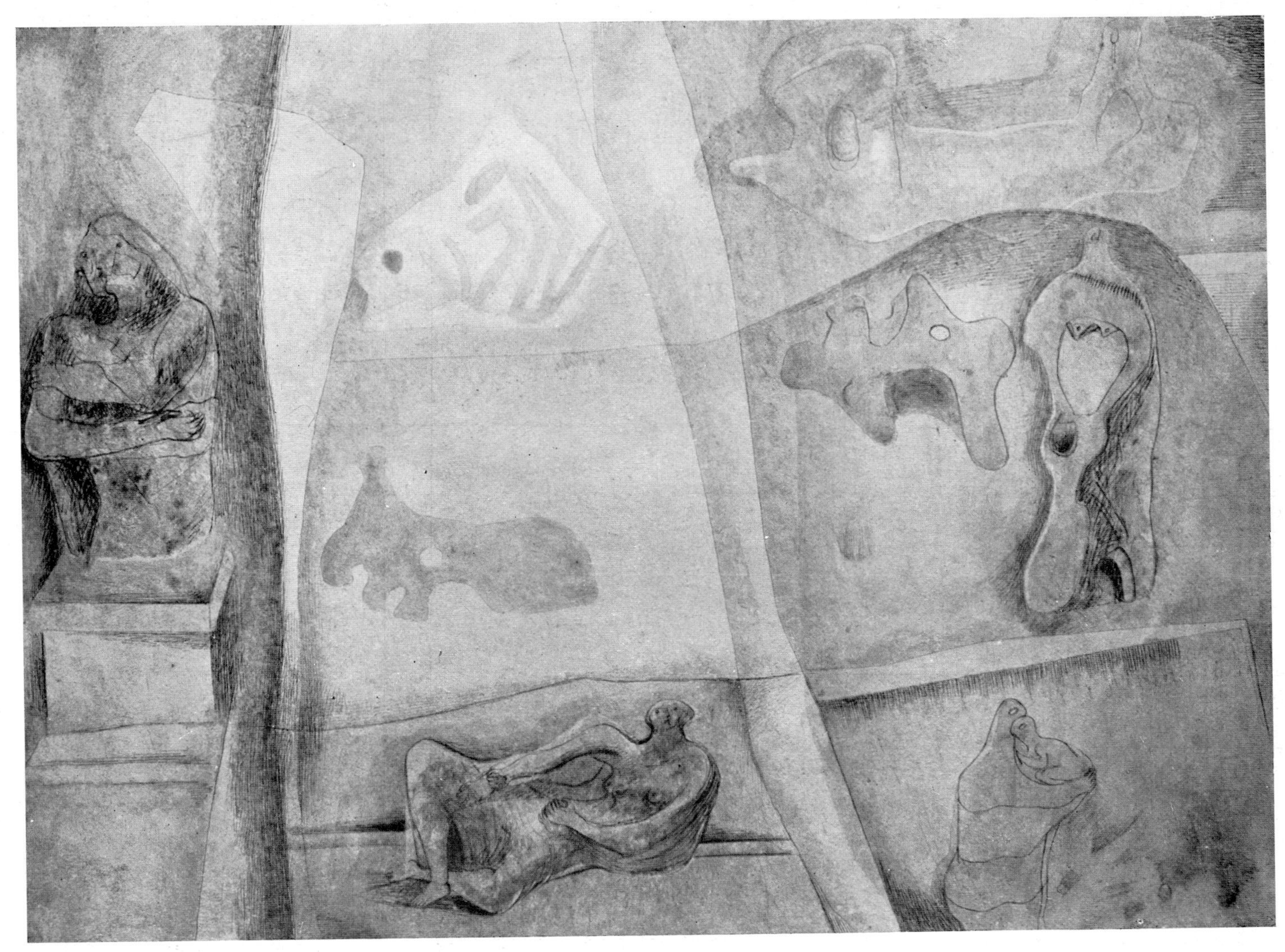

PLATE 6 DRAWING 1933

PLATE 7 DRAWING FOR STONE FIGURES 1937

PLATE 8 DRAWING FROM LIFE (SEATED FIGURE) 1935

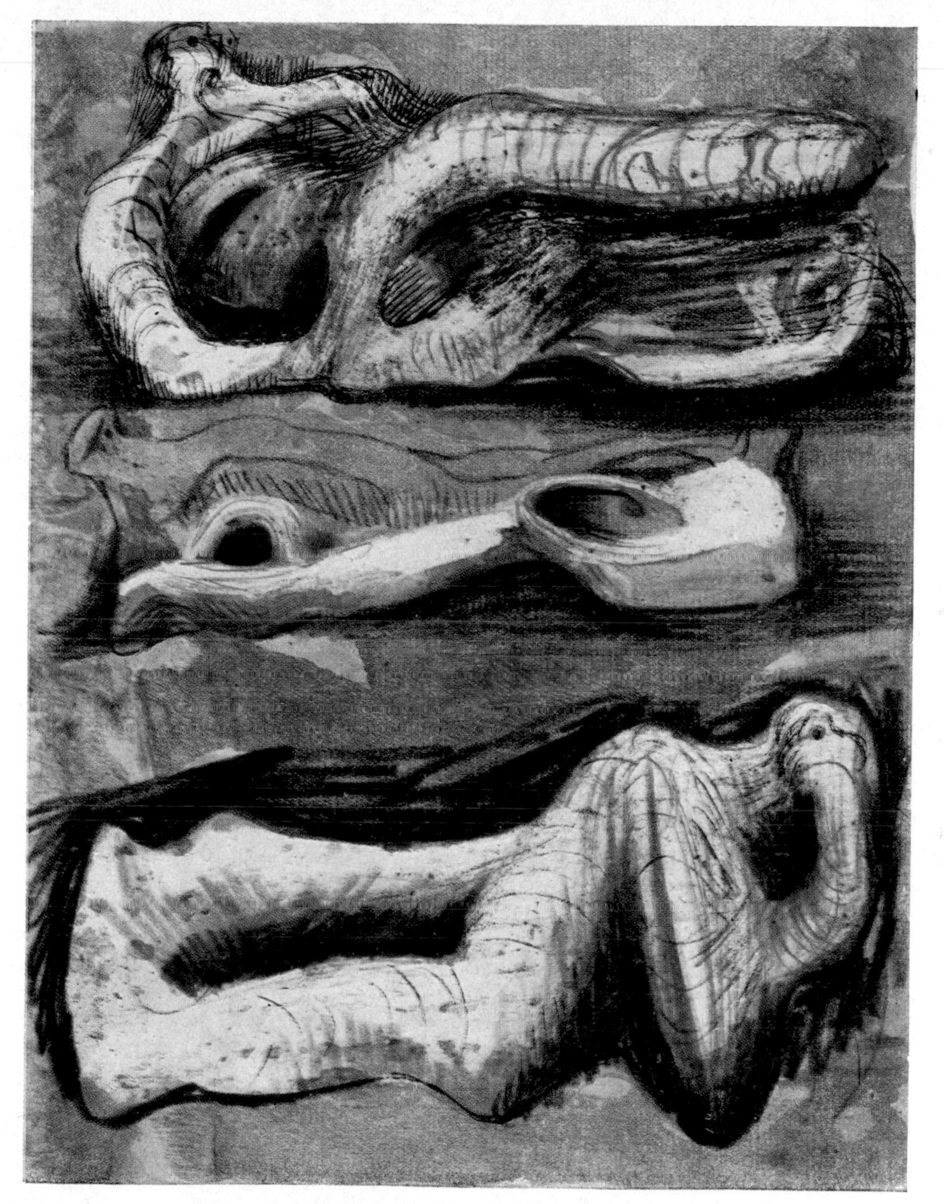

PLATE 9 IDEAS FOR SCULPTURE (SKETCH BOOK) 1941

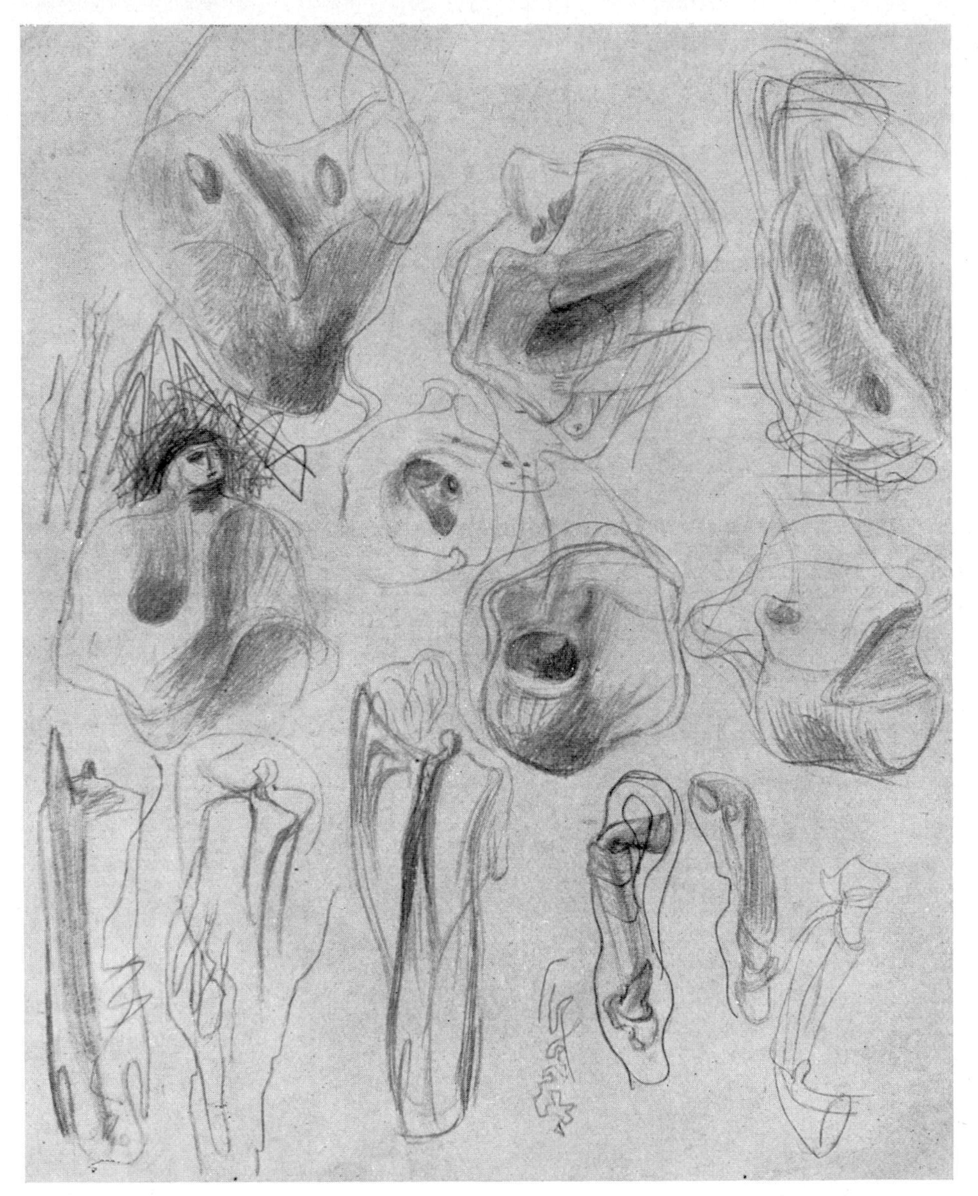

PLATE 10 SHAPES IN BONE (DRAWING FOR SCULPTURE) 1932

PLATE II TWO WOMEN SEATED 1940

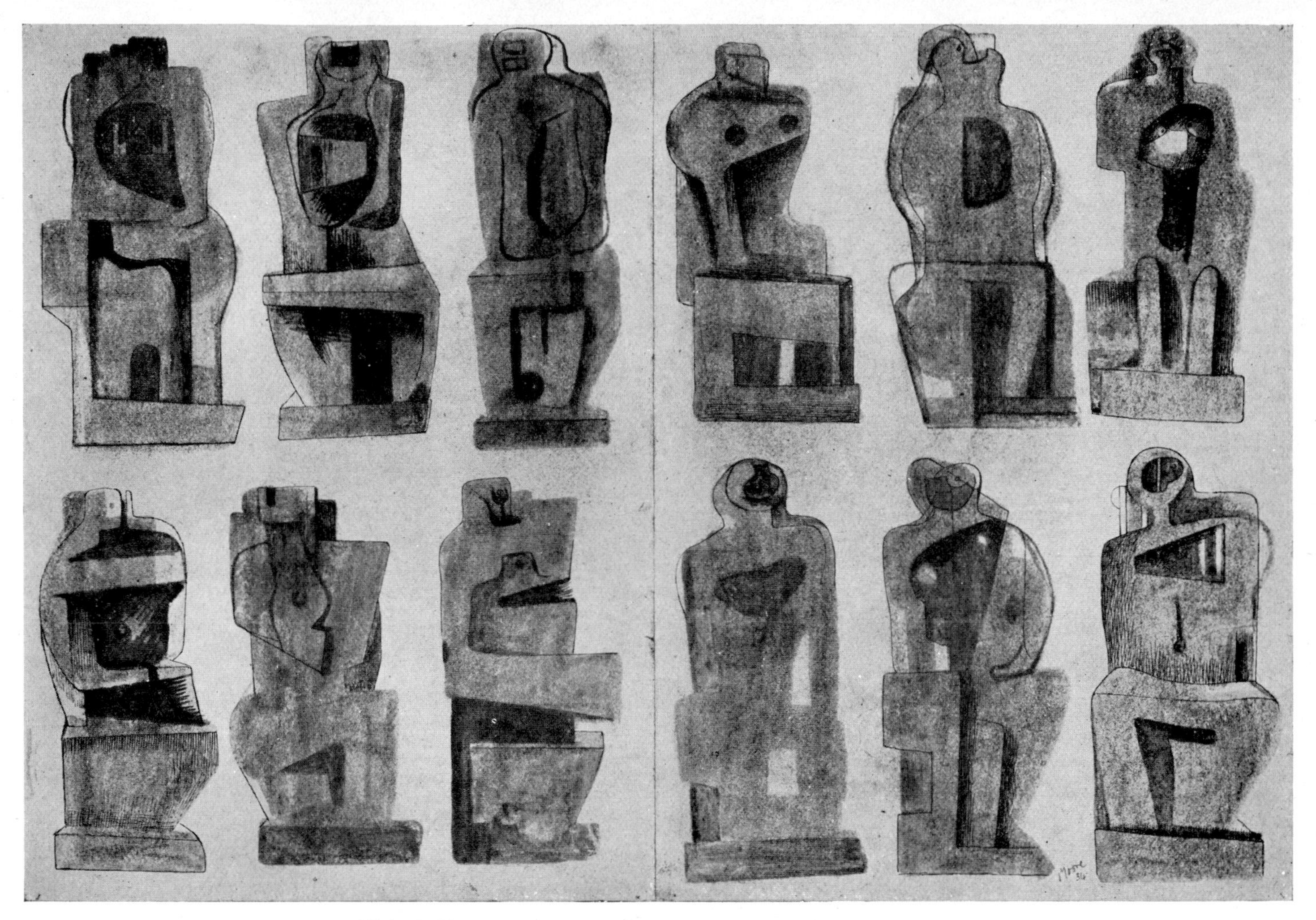

PLATE 12 SEATED FIGURES FOR STONE SCULPTURE 1934

PLATE 13 SEATED FIGURE AND POINTED FORMS 1940

PLATE 14 STANDING STONES IN LANDSCAPE 1936

PLATE 15 LANDSCAPE WITH FIGURES 1939

PLATE 16 DRAWING 1935

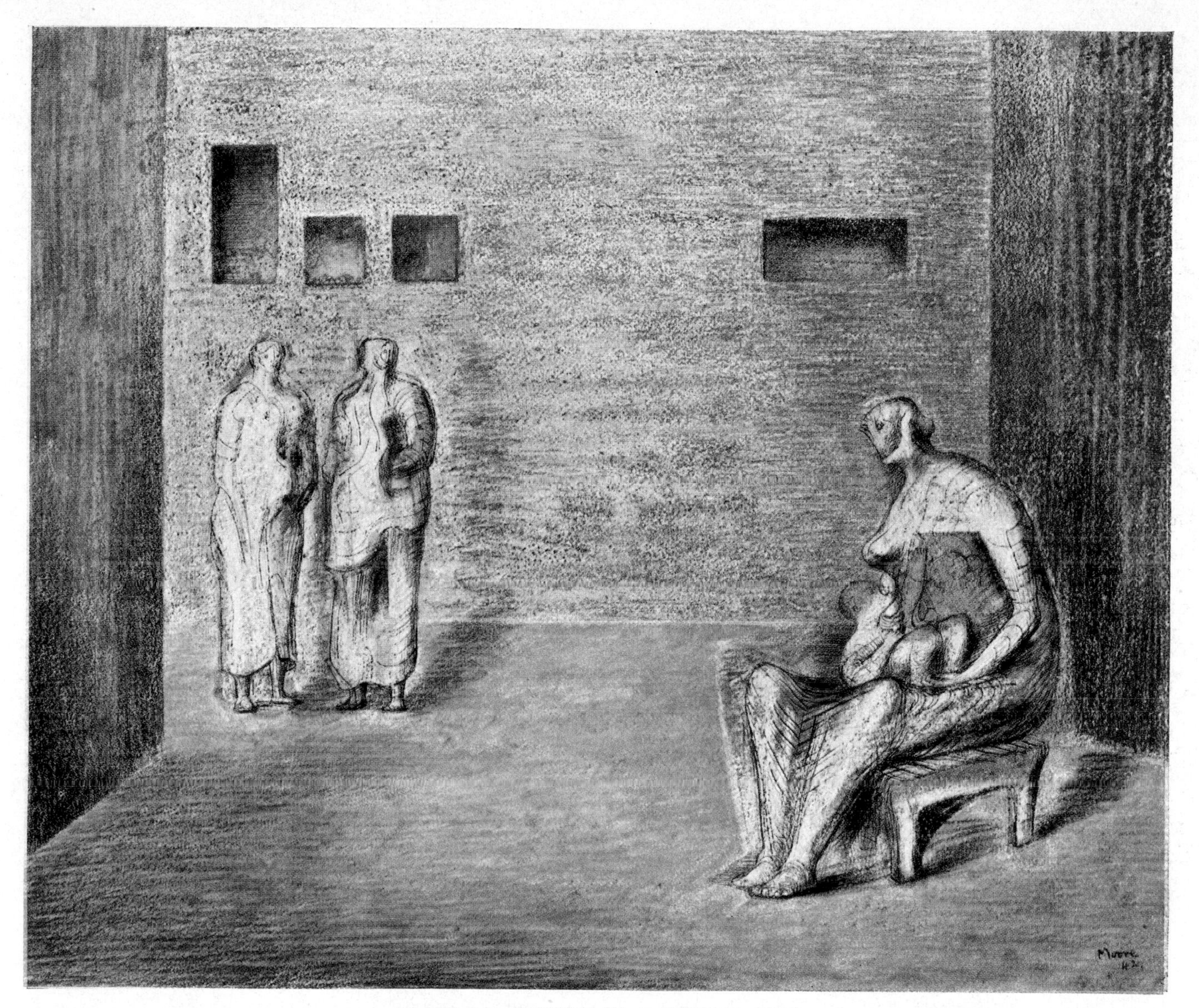

PLATE 17 FIGURES IN A SETTING 1942

PLATE 18 TWO WOMEN (DRAWING FOR SCULPTURE, COMBINING WOOD AND METAL) 1939

PLATE 19 RED ROCKS AND RECLINING FIGURE 1942

PLATE 20 OBJECTS (STRING AND WOOD) 1938

PLATE 21 FIGURES UNDER A BANK 1942

PLATE 22 RECLINING FIGURE 1938

PLATE 23 DRAPED FIGURES IN SHELTER 1941

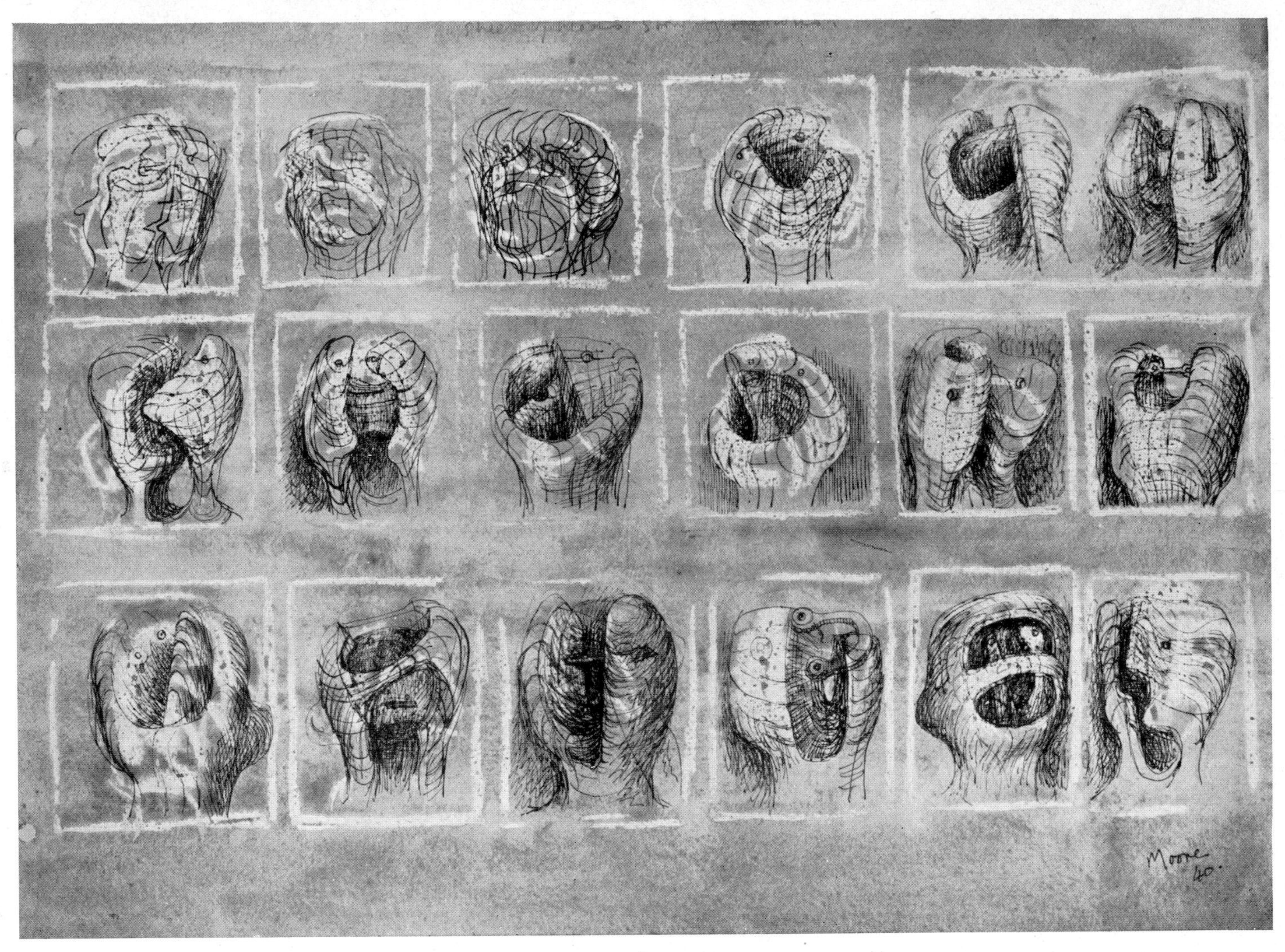

PLATE 24 PAGE OF HEADS (IDEAS FOR SCULPTURE) 1940

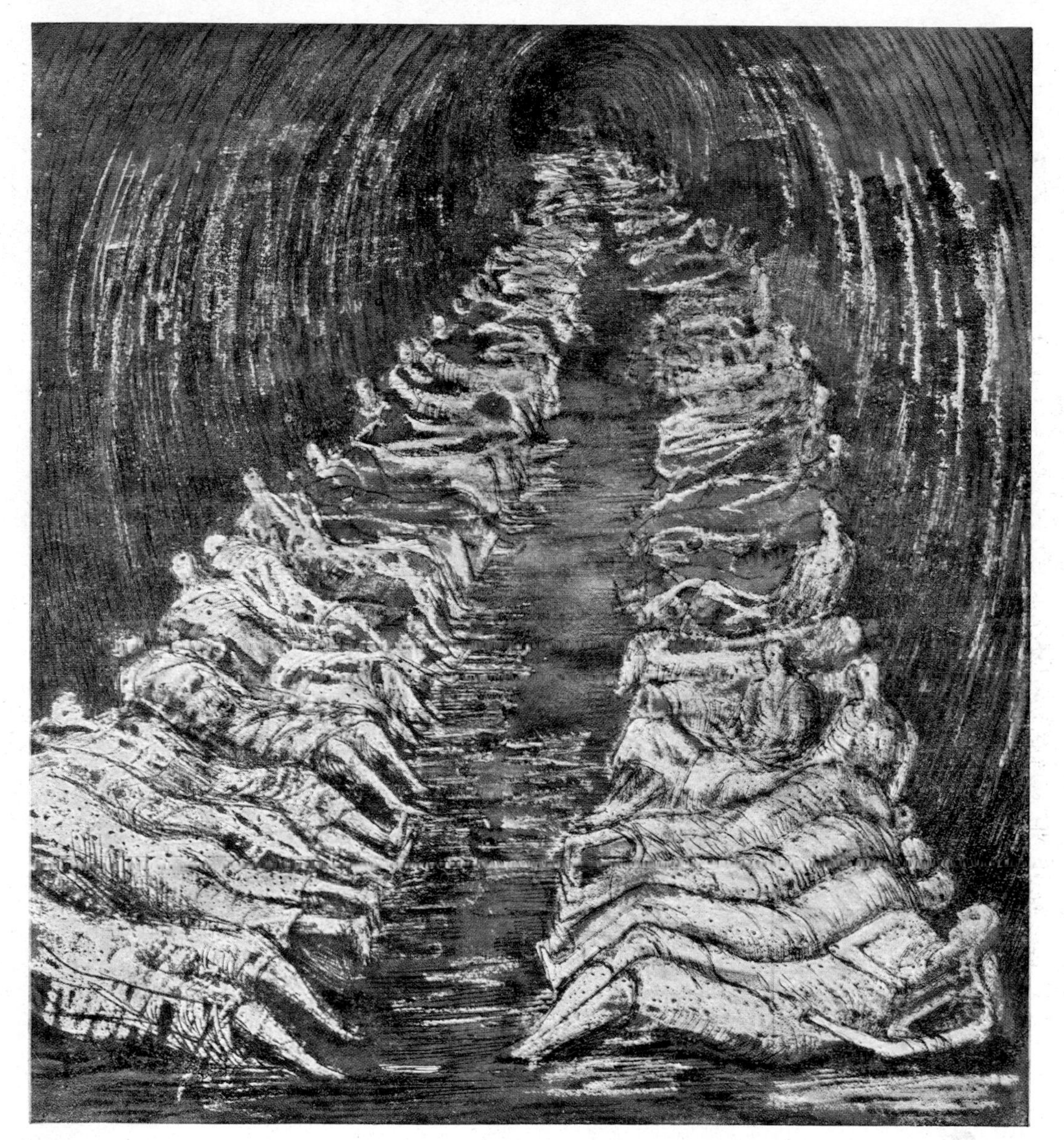

PLATE 25 TUBE SHELTER PERSPECTIVE 1941

PLATE 26 THREE WOMEN AND A CHILD 1940

PLATE 27 TWO WOMEN AND CHILD IN SHELTER 1940

PLATE 28 MINERS AT WORK ON THE COAL FACE 1942

PLATE 29 PINK AND GREEN SLEEPERS 1941

PLATE 30 ARRANGEMENT OF FIGURES 1942

PLATE 31 STUDY FOR RECLINING FIGURE IN WOOD 1940

PLATE 32 FOUR GREY SLEEPERS 1941